How
do I have
to be to... ?

Fergus Smith

B.Sc.(Hons), M.A., C.Q.S.W., D.M.S., Dip.M

10

6

18

21

CAe

Children Act Enterprises Ltd (CAE)
103 Mayfield Road
South Croydon
Surrey CR2 0BH

www.caeuk.org

© Fergus Smith 2005

British Library Cataloguing in Publication Data
A catalogue record for this book is available from the
British Library

ISBN 1 899986 02 2

Designed and typeset by Andrew Haig & Associates
Printed in the UK by The Lavenham Press

CAE is an independent organisation which publishes
guides to family and criminal law and provides
consultancy, research, training and independent
investigation services to the public, private and
voluntary sectors.

Index

Appendices

Introduction

■ This guide has been written for use by those who wish to know at what age (in England and Wales) a child or young person is allowed by law to undertake, or be held responsible for, a particular activity.

■ Like all other 'Personal Guides', it provides a simple yet accurate account of current legislation.

■ Readers can either consult the index where subjects are listed alphabetically or select a particular age from the following text to learn the rights and or responsibilities it brings with it.

■ Suggestions for additions to future editions are welcomed.

NB. Appendix 1 contains details of some useful organisations concerned with age-related rights and responsibilities of children and young people, and appendix 2 a list of all CAE publications.

Child/Young Person of Any Age

■ For some subjects covered in the 'any age' section, the law does not specify a particular age, or does not distinguish between children/young persons and adults.

Access to Personal Data

■ At any age a child/young person can apply for access to personal data held in manual records or on computers.

■ Regulations allow those who hold health, education or social work records some exemption from the obligation to provide access to the records if:

• Serious harm to the mental or physical health or condition of the applicant or any other person would be likely, if access were given [s.7 Data Protection Act 1998 and Data Protection (Subject Access Modification) Orders 2000)]

Alcohol – Confiscation

■ If an under 18 year old is found in a public place (or private place to which s/he has no right of access), consuming, or planning to consume alcohol (in a sealed or unsealed container) the Police may confiscate it [s.1 Confiscation of Alcohol (Young Persons) Act 1997 as amended by the Criminal Justice and Police Act 2001 and further amended by s.155 Licensing Act 2003].

Babysitting

■ There is no minimum age below which a child/young person may not lawfully baby-sit.

■ Those who have parental responsibility for the child must ensure the person asked to baby-sit is capable and will provide adequate care for the child otherwise both those with parental responsibility and the babysitter risk prosecution for cruelty or neglect, or even a civil action.

NB. The NSPCC recommend 16 as the minimum age for babysitting.

Borrowing Money

■ There is no minimum age limit to borrow money.

■ Potential lenders will be reluctant to risk their funds since any contract for repayment entered into by someone under 18 is un-enforceable [s.1 (b) Minor Contracts Act 1987].

Child Safety Order

■ The 'Child Safety Order' exists to protect children under 10 at risk of becoming involved in crime and may require a child to be at home at certain times or to stay away from certain places or people and be under the supervision of a responsible officer of the local authority or the Youth Offending Team (YOT) [s.11 Crime & Disorder Act 1998 as amended by s.60 Children Act 2004].

NB. Part 6 of Schedule 5 Children Act 2004 will remove the possibility of a Care Order being made where there has been a breach of a Child Safety Order.

Cinema

■ At the discretion of the person/s who have parental responsibility for her/him a child/young person of any age can see a 'U' or 'PG' certificate film.

Contact Order (see also s.8 Order)

■ If a court is satisfied that s/he has sufficient understanding, a child/young person of any age may be given leave (i.e. permission of the court) to apply for a 'Contact Order' [s.10 Children Act 1989].

■ A contact order as defined in s.8 Children Act 1989 will determine with whom s/he has a right of contact.

Contraception

■ There is no lower age limit to receive contraceptive advice or treatment from G.P.s or family planning clinics.

■ Doctors do not have to inform parents. They will break confidentiality only if they believe a young person is being abused and even then they should normally inform the young person of their intentions [*Confidentiality: Protecting and Providing Information* GMC 2004]

Contracts

■ A child of any age can theoretically enter into a valid contract for what are known as 'necessaries' e.g. food and clothing and a job, but cannot enter into a legally binding agreement for goods or services in exchange for money [s.3 Minors' Contracts Act 1987].

Counselling

■ There is no minimum age for the receipt of counselling (see also Medical Treatment).

Curfew Notice

■ Following consultation with one another and other relevant people, a local authority can impose a 'Child Curfew Notice' which for a maximum of 90 days:

  • Bans children/young persons aged less than 16 from being in a public place within a specified area, during specified hours between 9pm and 6am unless under effective control of a parent or responsible person aged 18or over [s.14 Crime and Disorder Act 1998 as amended by ss.48 & 49 Criminal Justice and Police Act 2001].

Dispersal of Groups

■ If police have reasonable grounds for believing the public is, or is likely to be intimidated, harassed, alarmed or distressed by a group of 2 or more under 16 year olds, and that anti-social behaviour is a significant and persistent problem in the area, the relevant officer will be able to authorise (for up to 6 months) a constable in uniform to:

- Direct the group to disperse
- Direct individuals/the group to leave the area
- Prohibit return within 24 hours [s.30(1)–(4) Anti-Social Behaviour Act 2003]

Emergency Protection Order

■ A child/young person of any age may, for up to 8 days be made subject of an 'Emergency Protection Order' (a court order which authorises her/his removal from risk or detention in a safe place) if s/he is otherwise likely to suffer significant harm [s.44 Children Act 1989].

NB. A court is unlikely to grant such an order on a person of 17 (or 16 if married) since once it expired the local authority would not be able to seek to get the young person committed to its care.

Evidence

■ In criminal proceedings a child is assumed to be a competent witness and her/his evidence is accepted un-sworn [s.33A Criminal Justice Act 1988 inserted by sch.9 para.33 Criminal Justice and Public Order Act 1994].

NB. Eligible witnesses aged less than 17 at time of a trial are entitled to special supportive measures [ss.16 & 17 Youth Justice and Criminal Evidence Act 1999].

■ In civil cases sworn evidence may be heard if the court is satisfied the child understands its meaning. Un-sworn evidence may be accepted if the court is satisfied the child understands s/he has a duty to tell the truth and has sufficient understanding to justify the evidence being heard [s.96 Children Act 1989].

Fruit Machines

■ No minimum age currently exists below which it is unlawful to play fruit/gaming machines.

NB. The government's draft Gambling Bill 2004 proposes to introduce measures to protect children and young people from risks associated with gambling.

Leaving Alone

■ There is no minimum age below which it is unlawful to leave a child alone, but **if** satisfied a child was suffering or likely to suffer 'significant harm' a court could impose an order which would authorise her/his removal (see Emergency Protection Order).

NB. The NSPCC suggests no child under 13 years of age be left unsupervised for more than brief periods.

Medical Treatment

■ If of 'sufficient understanding to make an informed decision', a child or young person of any age may give a valid **consent** to treatment [Gillick v West Norfolk & Wisbech Health Authority [1985] 3 All ER 402].

■ This does not give them the right to **refuse** treatment. A child/young person could not, for example override consent given by someone who has parental responsibility for her/him, or by a court.

Name Change

■ A child/young person of any age, if thought to understand the implications, can change her/his name by signing a 'statutory declaration'

■ If subject of a 'Residence Order' or a 'Care Order' a child's name cannot be changed without either the consent of everyone who has parental responsibility or a court [ss.13 & 33(7) Children Act 1989].

Passport

■ A child/young person of any age must have a passport of their own [Internationally Agreed Convention].

■ Children on a parent's passport as at October 5 1998 will not be affected until it is due for renewal, or the child reaches 16 years of age.

Police Powers of Protection

■ A child/young person of any age can be made subject of 'Police Powers of Protection' (which allow a constable to remove and accommodate her/him or ensure s/he remains where s/he is) if police believe s/he would otherwise suffer 'significant harm' [s.46 Children Act 1989].

Premium Bonds

■ A child/young person of less than 16 can have premium bonds in her/his name though their purchase must be completed by a parent/guardian, grandparent or great grandparent [Government Policy].

Prohibited Steps Order (see also s.8 Order)

■ If a court is satisfied s/he has sufficient understanding a child/young person of any age may be given leave (i.e. permission) to apply for a 'Prohibited Steps Order'.

■ A Prohibited Steps Order prevents anyone from taking any step which could be taken by a parent in meeting parental responsibility [s.10 Children Act 1989].

Religion

- A child/young person of any age who can make an informed decision may choose her/his own religion.

- A person who has parental responsibility could, if s/he believed the choice would be harmful, apply for a 'Prohibited Steps Order' (see index) or seek to make the child/young person a ward of High Court e.g. to prevent a child coming under the influence of an undesirable sect.

Residence Order (see also s.8 Order)

- If a court is satisfied s/he has sufficient understanding a child/young person of any age may be given leave (i.e. permission) to apply for a 'Residence Order' [s.10 Children Act 1989]. A Residence Order determines with whom the child/young person is to live.

s.8 (Children Act 1989) Orders (see also Contact, Prohibited Steps, Residence and Specific Issue Orders)

- If a court is satisfied s/he has sufficient understanding a child/young person of any age may be given leave (i.e. permission) to make an application for any of the s.8 Children Act Orders [s.10 Children Act 1989].

Smoking

■ A child/young person of any age can smoke. Under 16 year olds can have tobacco confiscated by police (or a uniformed park keeper) if found smoking in a street or public place [s.7 Children & Young Persons Act 1933].

Specific Issue Order (see also s.8 Orders)

■ If a court is satisfied that s/he has sufficient understanding a child/young person of any age may be given leave (i.e. permission) to make an application for a 'Specific Issue Order' [s.10 Children Act 1989]. A Specific Issue Order resolves a particular problem e.g. choice of schooling or need for medical treatment.

From Age 5

Alcohol

■ A child aged 5 and over may drink alcohol in private premises e.g. at home [s.5 Children & Young Persons Act 1933].

■ If the is child harmed, a parent/carer may be charged with a criminal offence for allowing her/him alcohol.

Cinema

■ An unaccompanied child of 5 can see a U or PG certificate film (may in London be required to be 7).

Fares

■ A child's fare is payable for those 5 or over on:

- Trains
- Buses and Tube trains in London [Conditions of Carriage London Transport]
- Buses in most other parts of England and Wales

School Attendance

■ A child of 5 must receive full-time education [s.8 (2) Education Act 1996].

■ Parent/s are obliged to ensure their children of compulsory school age receive efficient full-time education whether by regular attendance at school or otherwise [s.7 Education Act 1996].

Truants – Power to Remove

■ If a police officer finds a school age child of 5 years
 or over in a public place and has reasonable grounds
 for believing that the child is truanting, s/he can
 remove the child/young person and place her/him
 in school or in another designated premises [s.16(3)
 Crime and Disorder Act 1998].

From Age 7

Savings/Current Account

- A child of 7 and over can operate a National Savings account or purchase index-linked Savings Certificates [National Savings & Investments' Policy].

- A bank may allow a 7 year old to operate an account if satisfied s/he fully understands what s/he is doing.

From Age 10

Action Plan Order

- A child/young person of 10 and over may, if not already subject to one of a number of other court orders, be made subject of an 'Action Plan Order'

- An Action Plan Order compels the offender for a period of 3 months to meet a series of requirements as to activity, location and reparation [ss.69-72 Powers of Criminal Courts (Sentencing) Act 2000].

Anti-Social Behaviour Order

- An 'Anti-Social Behaviour Order' (ASBO) may be made by police, local authority or registered social landlord on a child of 10 or over if :

  - S/he has acted in a manner that caused or was likely to cause harassment, alarm or distress to 1 or more persons, not of the same household as her/himself **and**
  - Such an order is necessary to protect relevant persons within the relevant authority area [s.1(1A) Crime & Disorder Act 1998 as amended by s.61(1) Police Reform Act 2002 & s.85 Anti-social Behaviour Act 2003]

Attendance Centre

- If found guilty of an offence for which an adult could be imprisoned, a child of 10 or over may be ordered to attend a junior attendance centre for a maximum of twenty four hours [s.60 Powers of Criminal Courts (Sentencing) Act 2000].

Criminal Liability

- A child of 10 and over may be convicted of a criminal offence.

- An under 10 year old who behaves in a way that could lead to prosecution of a child 10 or over might be considered 'likely to suffer significant harm' as beyond parental control and be placed under supervision, or in care of a local authority (see Supervision and Care Orders).

- A 'Child Safety Order' might also be considered for such a child.

Curfew Order

- A court may make a child of 10 or over subject of a 'Curfew Order' requiring her/him to remain for specified time/s at a specified place (usually home) [ss.37-40 Powers of Criminal Courts (Sentencing) Act 2000].

  NB. The maximum duration of a Curfew Order is 6 months.

Detention During Her Majesty's Pleasure

■ If found guilty of murder a child/young person aged 10 or over may be detained indefinitely 'during Her Majesty's pleasure' [s.90 Powers of Criminal Courts (Sentencing) Act 2000].

Detention for a Specified Period

■ A child/young person of 10 to 17 may be sentenced to a period of detention not exceeding the maximum allowable in the case of a person aged 21 or over, if found guilty of:

- An offence which in the case of a person aged 21 or over carries a sentence of 14 years or more (other than one for which the sentence is fixed)
- Indecent assault on a woman
- Indecent assault on a man committed after September 30 1999 [s.91 (1); (3) Powers of Criminal Courts (Sentencing) Act 2000]

Penalty Notice

■ From the age of 10, an individual may be given a 'Penalty Notice' if s/he commits a range of low level disorderly conduct offences [effect of s.87 Anti-social Behaviour Act 2003 and The Penalties for Disorderly Behaviour (Amendment of Minimum Age) Order 2004].

■ Where a Penalty Notice is given to someone aged less than 16, a parent / guardian selected by the police is to be notified and becomes liable for payment

Police Detention

■ If arrested and detained by police a child/young person of 10 and over can be:

- Searched (including strip searched) and/or an intimate search of body orifices undertaken by a doctor or a registered nurse
- Fingerprinted
- Photographed
- Asked to provide non-intimate body samples e.g. hair or saliva

■ Intimate samples e.g. blood or semen will require parental consent if child is less than 14 and that of the young person and parent/s (if s/he is 14 or over).

■ A parent must be informed of the arrest/detention of a child/young person who has the right to communicate privately with a solicitor or inform someone else of her/his arrest, and to remain silent.

■ Child/young person must only be interviewed when a parent or other responsible person other than a police officer present [Police & Criminal Evidence Act 1984, Criminal Justice and Police Act 2001 current Code of Practice].

Rape etc

■ A boy of 10 or over may be charged with rape,
assault by penetration, sexual assault and causing a
person to engage in sexual activity without consent
[ss. 1 – 4 respectively Sexual Offences Act 2003].

Referral Order

■ A child/young person of 10 or over upon conviction,
must or may be referred to a 'Youth Offender Panel'
according to the crimes s/he has committed and the
circumstances.

■ The Youth Offender Panel will arrange a suitable
behaviour contract with the child/young person [Part
III Powers of Criminal Courts (Sentencing) Act 2000].

Remands to Local Authority Accommodation

■ Defendants of 10 to 16 inclusive, if refused bail, can
be remanded to accommodation which the local
authority is obliged to provide [s.23 Children and
Young Person's Act 1969 as substituted by
s.60.Criminal Justice Act 1991].

Supervision Order (Criminal)

■ If found guilty of a criminal offence a child of 10 to
17 inclusive may be made subject of a criminal
'Supervision Order' lasting up to 3 years [s.63 Powers
of Criminal Courts (Sentencing) Act 2000].

Work (part-time)

■ A child of 10 or over may, if local bye-laws say so, be employed on an occasional basis by a parent (who has to provide direct supervision), to do light agricultural/horticultural work [s.18 (2) & s.20 (2) Children and Young Person's Act 1933 as amended].

NB. The government has accepted recommendations by the 'Better Regulation Task Force' for substantial updating of laws about employment of children/young people and should, by February 2005 formally consult upon its proposals.

Youth Court

■ The Magistrates Court which deals with juvenile crime is known as the Youth Court and has jurisdiction over 10 to 17 year olds inclusive [ss.68;70 & Sch.8 Criminal Justice Act 1991].

From Age 12

Cinema

- A child of 12 and over may watch a '12 Certificate' film.

  NB. A child aged less than 12 may be admitted to a 12A film if accompanied by an adult.

Performance

- If the local authority grant her/him a licence, a child of 12 and over may be trained to participate in dangerous performances [s.24 Children & Young Person's Act 1933].

  NB. The maximum numbers of continuous hours per day any child (of 9 or over) may rehearse or participate in a performance is 9 [The Children (Performances) (Amendment) (no.2) Regulations 2000].

Pet Purchase

- A child of 12 and over may purchase a pet [s.3 Pet Animals Act 1951].

Remands to Secure Accommodation

■ A court can, if certain criteria are satisfied, remand to secure accommodation to be provided by the local authority:

- Boys or girls aged 12 to 14
- Girls aged 15 or 16

[s.23 (4) Children and Young Persons' Act 1969 as substituted by s.60 Criminal Justice Act 1991 and amended by s.97(1) Crime and Disorder Act 1998]

NB. 15 and 16 year old boys whose alleged or actual offences satisfy certain criteria and who are considered too vulnerable for prison must be placed in secure accommodation if it is available.

From Age 13

Secure Accommodation

■ A child of 13 to 17 inclusive who is 'looked after' by a local authority can, if certain criteria are met, be placed in a children's home which provides secure accommodation [s.25 Children Act 1989].

■ A child of less than 13 cannot be placed in secure accommodation without the permission of the Secretary of State for Health and Social Services [The Children (Secure Accommodation) Regulations 1991 as amended].

Work (part-time)

■ A child of 13 may undertake 'light' work only in jobs specified in local bye-laws for not more than 1 hour before school [s.18 Children and Young Person's Act 1933 as amended and the Children (Protection at Work) Regulations 1998].

■ Bye-laws (i.e. made by local authorities) are likely to specify 'permitted' employment as:

• Agricultural/horticultural work
• Newspaper delivery
• Shop work including shelf stocking
• Hairdressing salons
• Car washing by hand in a private residential setting
• Cafes

- Riding stables
- Domestic work in hotels

■ A local authority is also empowered to make bye-laws which:

- Distinguish between children of different ages, sexes, localities, trades, occupation and circumstances
- Prohibit specified occupations
- Prescribe minimum ages and numbers of hours in each day or week and times for which a child may be employed as well as meals and rest intervals and holidays plus other conditions

■ 'Light work' is work not likely to be harmful to safety or health and development of children or affect school attendance or ability to learn.

■ 'Prohibited employment' is likely to be defined by local authorities to include delivering milk, collecting money, work more than three metres above the ground, amusement arcades and personal care in residential care and nursing homes (unless under supervision of a responsible adult).

NB. The government has accepted recommendations by the 'Better Regulation Task Force' for substantial updating of laws about employment of children/young people and should, by February 2005 formally consult upon its proposals.

From Age 14

Air Weapon or Ammunition

- It is an offence to give an air weapon or ammunition to a child of less than 14 years of age [s.24 (4) Firearms Act 1968 as amended by s.38 (4) Anti-social Behaviour Act 2003].

  NB. Whilst it is not an offence for a young person of 14 and over to be in possession of an air weapon or ammunition if on private premises and with the consent if the occupier, s/he is committing an offence if s/he fires any missile beyond those premises.

Attendance Centre

- If found guilty of an offence for which an adult could be imprisoned, those aged 14 or over may be ordered to attend an attendance centre for a minimum of 12 hours and a maximum of 24 (which rises to 36 hours for those over 16 years of age) [s.60 Powers of Criminal Courts (Sentencing) Act 2000].

Detention for a Specified Period

- A 14 to 17 year old convicted for causing death by reckless driving or death by careless driving while under the influence of drink or drugs, may receive a fixed sentence of detention up maximum allowable for a person aged 21 or over [s.91 (2);(3) Powers of Criminal Courts (Sentencing) Act 2000].

Seatbelts

■ A young person of 14 or over is personally responsible for ensuring that (where they are fitted and must be worn) s/he uses a seat belt [s.14 Road Traffic Act 1988 & Motor Vehicles (Wearing of Seat Belts) Regulations 1993].

Work (part-time)

■ **So long as** s/he has a rest break of 1 hour every 4 hours, and a break of 2 consecutive weeks during a period in the year when not required to attend school, a young person of 14 or over may be employed (for light work only, paid or unpaid) outside of school hours:

  • For 2 hours or less between 7am – 7pm on school days and Sundays (and a maximum of 12 hours in a school week)
  • For up to 5 hours in any day which is not a school day or Sunday
  • For up to 25 hours per week in any week in which s/he is not required to attend school

■ A 14 year old may only engage in street trading if employed by her/his parent, directly supervised by them and licensed by the local authority [s.18 Children and Young Persons' Act 1933 as amended and Children (Protection at Work) Regulations 1998].

NB. 'Light work' = unlikely to be harmful to children's safety, health, development or affect school attendance or ability to learn. 'Prohibited employment' = delivering milk, collecting money, work more than three metres above ground, amusement arcades and personal care in residential care and nursing homes (unless under supervision of a responsible adult).

The government has accepted recommendations by the 'Better Regulation Task Force' for substantial updating of laws about employment of children/young people and should, by February 2005 formally consult upon its proposals.

From Age 15

Cinema

■ A young person of 15 or over can see a '15 Certificate' film at a cinema.

Detention and Training Order

■ A young person of 15 to 17 found guilty of an offence for which a person aged 21 or over could be imprisoned, may be sentenced to serve a minimum of 4 and a maximum of 24 months 'Detention and Training Order' [s.101(1);(2) Powers of Criminal Courts (Sentencing) Act 2000].

Work (part-time)

■ **So long as** s/he has a rest break of 1 every 4 hours, a break of 2 consecutive weeks during a period in year when not required to attend school, a young person of 15 may be employed (light work only) outside of school hours, for:

- 2 hours or less between 7am – 7pm on school days and Sundays (and for a maximum of 12 hours in a school week)
- Up to 8 hours a day on any day which is not a school day or Sunday
- Up to 35 hours per week in any week in s/he is not required to attend school

[S.18 Children & Young Person's Act 1933 as amended and the Children (Protection at Work) Regulations 1998]

NB. 'Light work' = unlikely to be harmful to safety or health or development of children or affect school attendance or ability to learn.

'Prohibited employment' is likely to be defined by local authorities to include delivering milk, collecting money, work more than three metres above the ground, amusement arcades and personal care in residential care or nursing homes (unless under supervision of a responsible adult).

The government has accepted recommendations by the 'Better Regulation Task Force' for substantial updating of laws about employment of children/young people and should, by February 2005 formally consult upon its proposals.

From Age 16

Aerosol Paint

- It is an offence to sell aerosol paint to anyone aged less than 16 [s.54 Anti-social Behaviour Act 2003].

Alcohol

- A young person of 16 may, for consumption with a meal in a pub or hotel and if accompanied by a person aged 18 or over, drink (but not buy), beer, wine or cider (but not spirits) [s.150 Licensing Act 2003].

Armed Forces

- A young person (of either sex) can (with parental consent) join the Armed Forces when s/he is 16 [Queen's Regulations as amended].

Community Punishment Order

- If found guilty of an offence for which an adult could be imprisoned a young person of 16 may be made subject of a 'Community Punishment Order' requiring her/him to do specified unpaid work [s.44 Criminal Justice and Court Services Act 2000].

Community Rehabilitation Order

■ At 16 a young person may be made subject of a Community Rehabilitation Order which can last from 6 months to 3 years [s.43 Criminal Justice and Court Services Act 2000].

Cruelty to Child

■ A young person of 16 may be charged with cruelty to a child of whom they have actual care [s.1 Children & Young Person's Act 1933].

Dental Treatment

■ Unless in full-time education a young person of 16 may be charged for certain dental treatment [National Health Service (Travelling and Remission of Charges) Regulations 1988].

Driving Licence

■ A 16 year old can hold a licence to drive a moped, mowing machine, tractor, invalid carriage, 'goped' or pedestrian controlled vehicle [s.101 Road Traffic Act 1988 & Motor Vehicle (Driving Licences) Regulations 1987].

Fares

■ A 16 year old is liable for full fares on buses and trains and on London tube trains [Conditions of Carriage (London Transport)]

Gliding

- At 16 a young person can be a pilot in command of a glider [Article 31 Air Navigation Order 2000]

Heterosexual Intercourse

- A young woman of 16 can lawfully consent to vaginal or anal intercourse with a male aged 16 or over and a young man to sexual intercourse with a female aged 16 or over [net effect of Sexual Offences legislation].

  NB. A boy or girl under 16 is not her/himself committing a criminal offence if s/he has intercourse with a male or female who is sixteen or over and who consents. However, the older person could be prosecuted for a variety of serious offences since a boy or girl aged less than 16 cannot give lawful (as opposed to factual) consent to sexual activity. In specified circumstances the older person might also be guilty of 'an abuse of a position of trust' (see index).

Homelessness

- A young person of 16 or 17 may in certain circumstances be entitled to accommodation from her/his local authority because either s/he is:

  - In 'priority need' as result of pregnancy, dependant child or otherwise vulnerable e.g. a learning disability [s.175- 178 & s.181-191 Housing Act 1996] or

- Assessed as 'in need' and her/his welfare would be seriously damaged without accommodation being provided [s.20(3) Children Act 1989]

■ A young person of 16 or 17 has an explicit right to overrule a parent who wishes to resume her/his care [s.20 (11) Children Act 1989].

NB. The Homelessness Act 2002 strengthens the duty of mutual co-operation between housing and social services authorities to advise and assist homeless persons aged 16 and 17.

Homosexual Intercourse

■ A male or female aged 16 or over can lawfully consent to homosexual acts (including anal intercourse) [net effect of Sexual Offences legislation].

NB. A boy or girl under 16 is not committing a criminal offence if s/he has intercourse with a male or female aged sixteen or over, and who consents. However, the older person could be prosecuted for a variety of serious offences since a boy or girl aged less than 16 cannot give lawful (as opposed to factual) consent to sexual activity. In specified circumstances the older person might also be guilty of 'an abuse of a position of trust' (see index).

Knives

■ It is an offence for a person to sell to a person under the age of 16 any:

- Knife, knife blade or razor blade, axe or other
- Article which has a blade or which is sharply pointed and which is made or adapted for use for causing injury to the person [s.141A Criminal Justice Act 1988 introduced by s.6 Offensive Weapons Act 1996]

NB. Whether a particular article is a knife is a question of fact, but using a wider definition this legislation prohibits sales of e.g. sheath knives, kitchen knives, craft knives and carpet knives to persons under the age of 16. This legislation does not apply to folding pocket knives if the cutting edge of the blade is less than 7.62cm, nor does it apply to replacement cartridges for safety razors, where less than 2mm of the blade is exposed.

The government is currently under pressure to raise to 18 the minimum age at which it is lawful to sell knives etc to young people.

Leaving Care

■ Any young person aged 16 to 21 (24 if in full-time education or training) who has been 'looked after' for a minimum aggregated period of 13 weeks since her/his 14th birthday, is entitled to have her/his needs assessed and met by the local authority who last looked after her/him [s.1 Children (Leaving Care) Act 2000].

Leaving Home

■ A 16 or 17 year old can leave home without parental consent but might be prevented in the case of a:

- 16 year old, by means of a successful application by the local authority for a Care Order or
- 16 or 17 year old, by being made a 'Ward of the High Court' [s.41 Supreme Court Act 1991]

Marriage

■ A young person of 16 can marry :

- With consent of both parents (if they are married or if an unmarried father has parental responsibility) or
- If a Residence Order exists, with consent of the holder of that order instead of the parent/s or
- If a Care Order exists, then with the consent of the relevant local authority as well as that of the parent/s [s.3 Marriage Act 1949 as amended]

■ If a young person of 16 or 17 marries without such consents the marriage is valid but s/he will have committed a criminal offence.

Medical Treatment

■ A young person of 16 may provide consent to surgical/medical/dental treatment. Unless grounds exist for believing s/he is mentally incompetent under the Mental Health Act 1983, no further consent is required [s.8 Family Law Reform Act 1969].

■ This does not give her/him the right to refuse treatment. S/he could not e.g. override consent given by someone who has parental responsibility for her/him or by a court.

NB. Consent to surgical/medical/dental treatment does not extend to the donation of blood or body organs.

Minimum Wage

■ 16 and 17 year olds inclusive were entitled from October 1 2004 to a minimum hourly rate of £3·00 [s.1 Minimum Wages Act 1998].

NB. This is the first time the national minimum wage has been extended to this age group.

Name Change

■ A 16 year old can record a new name by filing a deed poll with the High Court.

Optical Treatment

■ A 16 year old may be charged for both an eye test and optical treatment unless:

- In full-time education
- Any member of family is in receipt of income support
- Income is low or

- Eyesight is constantly changing [National Health Service (Optical Charges & Payments) Regulations 1989]

Passport

■ Subject to written parental consent, a 16 year old can apply for a passport. S/he can no longer travel on a parent's passport [Internationally Agreed Convention].

■ A parent's consent in unnecessary if the young person is married, or in the Armed Forces [Queen's Regulations].

Performance

■ A 16 year old can without a local authority licence:

- Participate in public performances or
- Train to take part in dangerous performances [s.37 Children & Young Person's Act 1933]

Prescription Charges

- A 16 year old may be charged with the cost of prescriptions unless:

  - In full-time education
  - Pregnant
  - In receipt of income support/family credit
  - On a low income or
  - In certain other limited circumstances [National Health Service (Charges for Drugs and Appliances) Regulations 1980].

Removal to Home by Police

- If, between 9pm and 6am a police officer in uniform finds a child/young person **aged less than 16** not under effective control of a parent or other person 18 or over, s/he may remove her/him to her/his home (unless the officer has reasonable grounds for thus suffer significant harm) [s.30(6) Anti-Social Behaviour Act 2003].

School Attendance

- A young person who is 16 during the 'school year' (i.e. including the summer holidays) can legally leave school on the last Friday in June [s.8 Education Act 1996].

- If her/his GCSEs finish earlier, the head teacher has discretion to allow her/him to leave before this date.

NB. The Education Maintenance Allowance (EMA) is a new direct, weekly payment to young people who remain in further education beyond the statutory school leaving age. Amounts range from £10 per week for households with incomes of approximately £30,000 to £30 for those whose incomes are below approximately £19,000 [rates stated as at April 2004], further information from www.dfes.gov.uk

Smoking

■ A 16 year old may lawfully buy cigarettes, tobacco and cigarette papers [s.7 Children & Young Person's Act 1933].

Work (full-time)

■ A 16 year old who has left school may work full-time (and obtain a national insurance number) [s.558 Education Act 1996].

■ Everyone over school leaving age who works and has a contract of employment is entitled, after 3 months, to 4 weeks paid holiday per year [Working Time Regulations 1998].

From Age 17

Air Weapons

■ A young person aged 17 or over may lawfully buy or possess an air weapon of a permissible type [s.22 Firearms Act 1968 as amended by s.38 Anti-social Behaviour Act 2003]

Blood Donation

■ At 17 a young person may donate her/his blood.

NB. Current policy of the Blood Transfusion Service.

Care Order

■ At 17 it is no longer possible for a court to make a Care Order.

■ Where a child is 16 or under and a court finds that s/he 'is suffering or likely to suffer significant harm', which is attributable to inadequate parental care or that the child is beyond parental control, it can make a Care Order which will mean that (potentially until the child/young person is 18) the local authority shares parental responsibility with parents and can decide where s/he shall live [s.31 Children Act 1989].

NB. A 'Care Order' cannot be made on a young person of 16 who is or has been married.

Driving Licence

■ At 17 a young person may hold a driving licence to drive a:

- Motorbike (with specified restrictions as to engine size and power)
- 3 wheeler car, tricycle or van (up to a weight of 550Kg unladen)
- Car or van (manual or automatic) with up to a total of 9 seats and maximum weight of 3,500Kg (including any trailer) [s.101 Road Traffic Act 1988].

Flying

■ A 17 year old may obtain a private pilot's licence to fly a plane, gyro plane, helicopter, balloon or airship [Sch.8 Air Navigation Order 2000].

Supervision Order (Welfare)

■ At 17 it is no longer possible for a court to make welfare Supervision Order.

■ If a court finds that a child/young person of up to and including 16 'is suffering or likely to suffer significant harm', which is attributable to inadequate parental care they can make a Supervision Order to the local authority which will mean that for at least 12 months, the child/young person will be advised, assisted and befriended and, together with their parent/current caregiver must comply with directions given by the supervising officer [s.31 Children Act 1989].

From Age 18

*AN 18 YEAR OLD HAS REACHED THE AGE OF
MAJORITY AND BECOMES AN ADULT AS FAR AS
THE LAW IS CONCERNED [s.1 Family Law Reform
Act 1969]*

Abuse of Position of Trust

■ A person aged 18 or over can be prosecuted if s/he
is in a 'position of trust' with respect to a person less
than 18 years of age and:

- Participates in sexual activity with her/him
- Causes or incites the child/young person to
  engage in sexual activity
- Engages in sexual activity in the presence of the
  child/young person
- Causes a child/young person to watch a sexual
  act [ss. 16–19 Sexual Offences Act 2003]

■ A person is in a 'position of trust' if s/he looks after,
i.e. is regularly involved in caring for, training,
supervising or being in sole charge of a person aged
less than 18, as defined in s.22 Sexual Offences Act
2003 [see companion CAE guide to the SOA 2003]

*NB. The SOA 2003 is intended to protect vulnerable
young people from exploitation. It is a defence if the
older person can satisfy the court s/he did not know
the younger person was less 18, or that s/he was in a
'position of trust', or that s/he was lawfully married to
the younger person.*

Adoption

■ A person of 18 or over cannot be adopted.

■ Someone who has been adopted can apply to:

- The Registrar General for a copy of her/his original birth certificate [s.51 Adoption Act 1976]
- Place her/his name and address on the adoption contact register [s.51A Adoption Act 1976]

NB. The Adoption and Children Act 2002 is likely to be fully implemented by late 2005 and will change the above provisions.

Alcohol

■ At 18 a young person may buy and consume alcohol in a pub or a bar [consequences of s.149 Licensing Act 2003].

NB. A person aged less than 18 commits no offence if s/he tries to buy alcohol at the request of police or weights and measures officers i.e. has been engaged to test the responses of local off-licences and pubs etc [s.149(2) Licensing Act 2003].

Armed Forces

■ At 18 a young person can join the Armed Forces without parental consent.

Betting

- An 18 year old can enter a betting shop and place a bet [s.21 Betting, Gaming and Lotteries Act 1963].

- An under 18 year old is allowed to enter a bingo club so long as s/he does not participate in a game.

Cinema

- At 18 a young person may see an '18' rated film.

Contracts

- An 18 year old may enter contractual arrangements and thus:

  - Buy property
  - Sue and be sued
  - Act as an executor/administrator of the estate of a dead person

Dental Treatment

- An 18 year old can be charged for dental treatment unless still in full-time education or pregnant [National Health Service (Travelling Expenses and Remission of Charges) Regulations 1988].

Driving Licence

- At 18 a young person may hold a licence to drive a vehicle between 3,500Kgs and 7,500Kgs [s.101 Road Traffic Act 1988].

Fireworks

- A young person of 18 may lawfully buy fireworks [s.31 Explosives Act 1875 & para.7 Fireworks (Safety) Regulations 1997].

- At 18, the prohibition of possession of an adult firework in a public place [Fireworks Act 2003 and Fireworks Regulations 2004] no longer applies.

   NB. It is not an offence for under 18s to possess caps, cracker snaps and party poppers.

Flying

- A young person of 18 can obtain a commercial pilot's licence to fly a glider, aeroplane, helicopter, gyro plane, balloon or airship [Sch.8 Air Navigation Order 2000].

Hypnotism

- At 18 a young person may participate in a hypnotic show [s.3 Hypnotism Act 1952]

Jury Service

- An 18 year may serve on a jury [s.1 Juries Act 1974].

Minimum Wage

- 18 to 21 year olds **inclusive** are entitled from October 1 2004 to a minimum hourly rate of £4-10 [s.1 Minimum Wages Act 1998].

Mortgage

- An 18 year old may take out a mortgage.

Solvents

- It is an offence for a shop to sell solvents to anyone under 18 if it is considered the product may be abused by the person [s.1 Intoxicating Substances Supply Act 1985].

- It is also an offence to sell to under 18 year old, gas lighter refills [s.11 Consumer Protection Act 1987].

Tattoo

- At 18 a young person may be tattooed without parental consent [s.1 Tattooing of Minors Act 1969].

Tissue/ Body Donation

- At 18 a young person can, without parental consent:

  - Bequeath tissues for transplant purposes or
  - Donate her/his body to medical science

Voting

- At 18 a young person may vote in local, general and European elections [ss.1 (1) (c) & 2(1) (c) Representation of the Peoples Act 1983].

Will

- An 18 year old can make a valid will [s.7 Wills Act 1837].

- Special arrangements exist to enable under 18 year olds who are in the Armed Forces to make a will [s.1 Wills (Soldiers and Sailors) Act 1918].

From Age 21

Adoption

- At 21, it becomes possible to adopt a child [s.14 Adoption Act 1976]

- An 'Adoption Order' can be made in favour of a married couple (one of whom is the actual parent and at least 18) and the other 21 years of age.

  NB. All provisions of the Adoption and Children Act 2002 are likely to come into force by the end of 2005 and will substantially change the current law relating to adoption.

Councillor

- At 21, it is possible to become a local councillor [s.79 Local Government Act 1972].

Driving Licence

- A 21 year old may hold a licence to drive a:

  - Any size motor bike with or without a sidecar
  - Medium sized vehicle with a trailer (maximum weight inclusive of trailer 1,200Kgs)
  - Large vehicle (over 3,500Kgs) with a trailer up to 750Kgs
  - Bus
  - Road Roller [s.101 Road Traffic Act 1988]

Member of Parliament

■ At 21, it is possible to become a Member of
Parliament [s.7 Parliamentary Elections Act 1695].

Prison

■ If given a custodial sentence a 21 year old will be
placed in prison rather than a young offenders'
institution [effect of s.96 Powers of Criminal Courts
(Sentencing) Act 2001].

Appendix 1 – Useful Contacts

CitizenCard

- Backed by Home Office and Department of Health, 'Citizencard' issues to children aged 6 and over, resident in the UK, 'proof of age' cards.

- Call 0870 240 1221 or visit www.citizencard.net

Children's Legal Centre

- Advice line and e-mail service at www.clc.live.poptech.coop

Childline

- Offers a confidential help-line for young people who are worried or frightened or just need someone to talk to.

- Call (free) 24 hours a day 0800 1111

Runaway Helpline

- A national free-call help-line for those aged 17 and under who have run away or been forced to leave home so that they can send a message to their family or seek confidential help and advice.

- Call (free) 24 hours a day 0808 800 70 70 or contact via www.runawayhelpline.org

  See also: www.need2know.co.uk the government funded all purpose web portal for young people

Appendix 2: CAE Publications

■ Personal Guides:
- Children Act 1989 in The Context of Human Rights Act 1998
- Children Act 2004
- Child Protection
- Residential Care of Children
- Fostering
- 'How Old Do I Have To Be?' (a simple guide to the rights and responsibilities of 0–21 year olds)
- Domestic Violence (Part IV Family Law Act 1996 & Protection from Harassment Act 1997)
- Looking After Children: Good Parenting, Good Outcomes (DH LAC System)
- Crime and Disorder Act 1998
- Sexual Offences Act 2003
- Anti Social Behaviour

Available from: Children Act Enterprises Ltd,
103 Mayfield Road, South Croydon, Surrey CR2 0BH
tel: 020 8651 0554 fax: 020 8405 8483
email: childact@dial.pipex.com

www.caeuk.org

Discounts for orders of 50 or more of any one title